Horses

Horses

Mary Ann McDonald

THE CHILD'S WORLD®, INC.

Library of Congress Cataloging-in-Publication Data
McDonald, Mary Ann.
Horses/written by Mary Ann McDonald.
p.   cm.
Includes index.
Summary: An introduction to the physical characteristics,
behavior, and life cycle of horses.
ISBN 1-56766-377-X (smythe-sewn, lib, reinforced)
1. Horses—Juvenile literature. [1. Horses.] I. Title.
SF302.M27   1997
636.1—DC21   96-46191
CIP
AC

Photo Credits

COMSTOCK/Art Gingert: 9
COMSTOCK/COMSTOCK, Inc: 2, 19, 26
COMSTOCK/Denver Bryan: 13
COMSTOCK/Gary J. Benson: 15
COMSTOCK/Georg Gerster: 24
COMSTOCK/Townshend P/ Dickinson: 16
DPA/DEMBINSKY PHOTO ASSOC: 6
Joe McDonald: 29, 30
Kevin Schafer: 23
Patrisha Thomson/Tony Stone Images: 10
Patrick Cone: cover
William A. Muñoz: 20

On the cover...

Front cover: This *pinto* stallion is standing in a field.
Page 2: These horses like to run in the early morning sunshine.

Table of Contents

Imagine that you are on a farm, sitting in a field of grass. The wind is rustling the leaves in the trees. The sun is shining on the wildflowers. Grasshoppers and crickets are jumping in the air. The farmer's cat is climbing up a tree. Farther out in the field, you see a large animal walking in the grass. What could this animal be? It's a horse!

This horse is running in a field.

What Do Horses Look Like?

Horses are large, powerful animals with four strong legs. They have a long neck that can bend down to the ground. They have two large eyes that can see in many directions. They also have hair on their foreheads and down their necks. This long hair is called a **mane**. Horses have a long tail, too. It swishes back and forth to keeps bugs away.

A horse's long neck can bend all the way to the ground.

A horse's foot is very strange—it's like one large toe! The front of the toe has a hard covering called a **hoof**. The hoof is like your toenail, but much bigger and harder. Hooves help the horse run and change directions quickly.

Many horses wear **horseshoes** to help them walk on hard surfaces. Horseshoes aren't anything like your own shoes. They're U-shaped pieces of metal that are nailed to the hoof! Nailing the shoes on doesn't hurt—it feels just like clipping your fingernails. Without horseshoes, the horse's hooves would crack and split, and that would hurt a lot.

This horse wears horseshoes and special wrappings to protect its legs.

What Are Baby Horses Like?

Adult female horses are called **mares**. A mare usually has only one baby at a time. The baby is called a **foal**. The foal can stand and walk on its own when it is just a few hours old! Foals look like adult horses, but much smaller. Foals like to run and play.

When a foal is very young, it isn't ready to eat grass. So what does it eat? The mare makes milk in her body, just like a cow. Until the foal is about three weeks old, all it eats is its mother's milk. But after it watches its mother for a while, it starts to nibble on grass.

This *Appaloosa* foal is standing by its mother while she eats some grass.

When the baby is about a year old, it isn't called a foal anymore. If the young horse is a female, it is called a **filly**. If it is a male, it is called a **colt**. Colts and fillies keep growing until they are about five years old.

This *thoroughbred* filly is about a year old.

Horses love to eat grass and other plants. Alfalfa is one of their favorite plants. They like to eat dried grass, called hay. They also eat grains such as oats, barley, and corn. Carrots and apples are favorite treats.

These wild horses are eating grasses in a field.

Where Do Horses Live?

During the cold winter months, horses that live on farms stay inside a barn. Inside the barn, each horse has its own little room, called a **stall**. The stalls are full of straw for the horses to sleep on.

In warm weather, horses live outside. They run and play in large fields called pastures. The pastures are full of grasses and plants for the horses to eat. Some horses even like to sleep in their pastures.

These horses can run and play all day in their grassy pasture.

Are There Different Kinds of Horses?

People raise horses of many different colors and sizes. Each different kind is called a **breed**. There are almost 200 different breeds of horses around the world. Some breeds are brown or black. Others are white with spots. **Ponies** are some of the smallest breeds. They weigh only about 400 pounds. The largest breeds are *draft horses*. They are also called "work horses." They can weigh almost 2,000 pounds! These big horses were bred to pull wagons and plows.

These *draft horses* are working hard in a field.

In some parts of the world, horses still live in the wild. One kind of wild horse is the *Przewalski* (sheh-VAHL-skee) *horse*. It lives in Mongolia, a country near China. Another kind of wild horse has stripes! Can you guess what it is? It's the *zebra*, a wild horse that lives in Africa.

A *zebra* has black and white stripes.

In parts of the western United States, *mustangs* still run free. Mustangs are horses that escaped from early settlers. The mustangs travel in groups called **herds**. Each herd is controlled by an adult male horse. Adult male horses are called **stallions**. Stallions are very strong. Wild stallions can be dangerous.

A herd of *mustangs* runs across the prairie.

What Are Horses Used For?

Long ago, people began using horses to help them work. They trained horses to pull heavy loads and carry important things. Horses were used to plow fields and harvest crops. They were even taught to carry people from one place to another.

This horse has been taught to pull a buggy.

Today, we don't need horses as much as we used to. We drive cars instead of riding horses. Farmers use tractors to plow their fields. But in some parts of the world, horses are still used every day. In some countries, people don't have many tractors or cars. They still use horses to pull plows and wagons full of hay. And sometimes people still ride them to get from place to place.

This horse is pulling a buggy in a race.

Horses are very friendly and clever animals. They have good memories and can learn many tricks. Some horses learn to race, jump, and pull carts and wagons. Others are raised to be judged in contests. And some horses just live as pets. Horses will always be an important part of our lives. In play or in work, horses are good friends to people.

This *Palomino horse* is standing in the sunshine.

Glossary

breed (BREED)
A breed is one kind of an animal. There are almost 200 breeds of horses.

colt (KOLT)
A colt is a young male horse after it is about a year old.

filly (FIH-lee)
A filly is a young female horse after it is about a year old

foal (FOHL)
A baby horse under a year old is called a foal. Foals have long legs and love to play.

herd (HERD)
A herd is a group of horses. A herd is controlled by a stallion.

hoof (HOOF)
A hoof is the hard covering on the front of a horse's foot. It is like a big, strong toenail.

horseshoes (HORS–shooz)
Horseshoes are U-shaped pieces of metal that protect a horse's foot.

mane (MAIN)
A mane is the long hair that grows on a horse's forehead and neck.

mare (MAIR)
A mare is an adult female horse.

pastures (PAS-churz)
Pastures are large, grassy fields. Horses eat, sleep, and play in pastures.

ponies (POH-nees)
Ponies are very small kinds of horses.

stall (STAHL)
A room in a barn where a horse lives is called a stall.

stallion (STAL-yun)
A stallion is an adult male horse.

Index